Color AROUND US

by Lara Whitehead

Rigby PM Plus Nonfiction Sapphire Level
The Science of Cooking
Built Like That
Color Around Us
Fibers in Fashion
Making Shapes
Measure for Measure

Rigby PM Plus Nonfiction
part of the Rigby PM Program
Sapphire Level

U.S. edition © 2004 Rigby Education
A division of Reed Elsevier Inc.
Harcourt Achieve Inc.
10801 N. MoPac Expressway
Building #3
Austin, TX 78759
www.harcourtachieve.com

Text © 2003 Thomson Learning Australia
Illustrations © 2003 Thomson Learning Australia
Originally published in Australia by Thomson Learning Australia

All rights reserved. No part of this publication may be reproduced or transmitted in any form or by any means, electronic or mechanical, including photocopying, recording, taping, or any information storage and retrieval system, without permission in writing from the publisher.

10 9 8 7 6 5 4 3 2
07 06 05

Color Around Us
    ISBN 0 7578 6950 5

Printed in China by 1010 Printing Limited

Acknowledgements:
Photographs by **AAP Image**, p. 16 right; **Australian Picture Library**/ Corbis/ Bettmann, p. 7 bottom/ Dan Guravich, p. 28 bottom left/ David Keaton, p. 6-7; **Getty Images**/ Imagebank, p. 16 left/ PhotoDisc, pp. 4, 5; **PhotoDisc**, p. 21 right; **Eric Schlögl**, p. 29; **Stock Photos**, pp. 28 bottom right, 30, 31; **Bill Thomas**, front cover, pp. 14, 17, 18, 19, 20.

Contents

Chapter 1	Color My World	4
Chapter 2	Discovering Hidden Colors	6
Chapter 3	Surfing the Light Waves	10
Chapter 4	Seeing Color	14
Chapter 5	So You Want Pink Hair?	16
Chapter 6	Foods, Moods, and Marketing	20
Chapter 7	The Color of the Weather Report	24
Chapter 8	Sarah Snap's Field Notes	28
Chapter 9	At the Printer	30
Glossary		32
Index		33

Chapter 1

Color My World

For most of us, the world we see every day is made up of colors and light. Yellow flowers, blue sky, and red apples seem normal to our eyes.

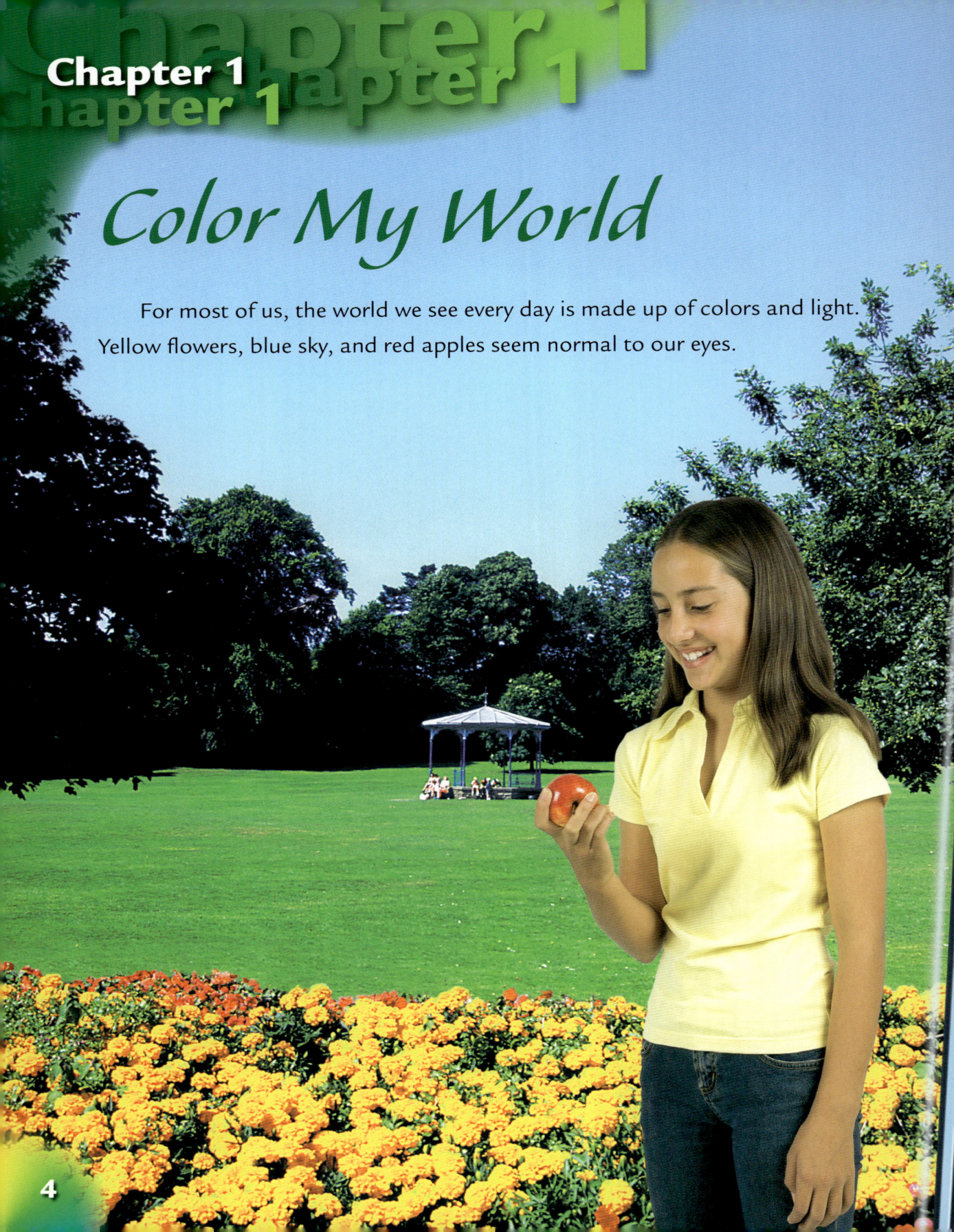

Colors affect our moods and feelings and the decisions we make. So, what if the colors were different? Would you notice if your apple were blue or the sky turned green? What makes color anyway?

Chapter 2

Discovering Hidden Colors

Sunlight is around us every day. We don't notice it because it seems invisible. It's hard to believe, then, that hidden inside every ray of sunlight is a rainbow of colors.

The first person to discover this was the English scientist Sir Isaac Newton. Newton was born in 1642 and died in 1727. When he was twenty-five years old, he started experimenting with beams of sunlight coming in through his windows.

Did You Know?

As a young man Newton made three of the most important discoveries in the history of science — and all within eighteen months. Along with his discoveries of light and color, Newton created the theory of gravity and invented a new type of mathematics, called calculus.

The London News

August 15, 1666

Newton Discovers Fabulous Colors in Light!

Fabulous colors are hiding in ordinary sunlight, according to the young scientist Isaac Newton. A few months ago, Newton left his teaching job at Cambridge University and returned to his home in the country, where he started doing some experiments.

One day Newton closed the curtains in his room and shut out all of the light except for a small sunbeam that was coming through a crack. Next he held up a piece of cut glass, called a **prism**. Newton moved the prism so that the beam of light shone through it. Instantly a rainbow of colors appeared on the opposite wall.

As he turned the prism, the band of little rainbow colors moved too. Newton had **splintered** the white light into seven separate colors.

Newton continued with his experiments. He tried to make just one of the rainbow colors — red — pass through a second prism. He wanted to see if red was made up of any other colors, too. It wasn't. No matter which color he tried, none of the rainbow colors would splinter any more. With these experiments Newton now claims that the colors are in the white light itself, and are not produced by the prism.

The Colors of the Spectrum

Spectrum is the name given to the band of colors that make up white light. The colors of the spectrum are red, orange, yellow, green, blue, indigo, and violet.

This is how Newton's experiment works.

White light shines through a prism, and is splintered into the colors of the spectrum.

Did You Know?

It's easy to remember the colors in the spectrum.
Just think ROY–G–BIV!
Red, Orange, Yellow – Green – Blue, Indigo, Violet.

One color from the spectrum, red, shines through a hole in a notecard, and then through a second prism. The red beam cannot be split into any more colors.

9

Chapter 3

Surfing the Light Waves

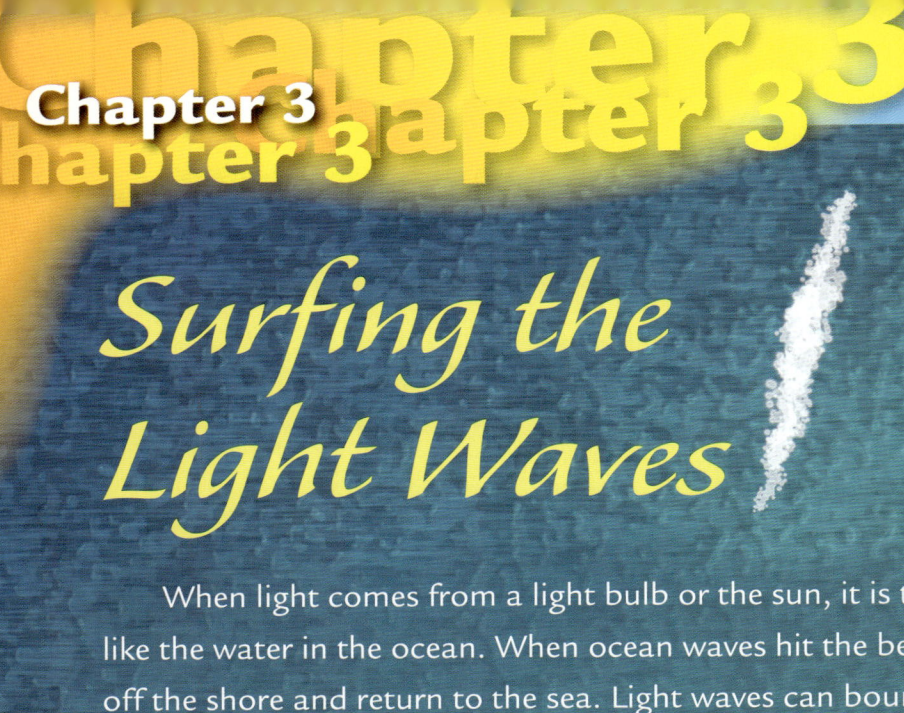

When light comes from a light bulb or the sun, it is traveling in waves, like the water in the ocean. When ocean waves hit the beach, they bounce off the shore and return to the sea. Light waves can bounce off objects, too. The waves that bounce away get reflected into our eyes. Every color in the spectrum has a different wavelength. Violet has the shortest wavelength, and red has the longest.

We see different colors around us because of the way that objects **absorb**, **reflect**, or **transmit** the waves of light that hit them.

A black surfboard absorbs all of the light that hits it. All seven of the spectrum colors are absorbed, so nothing is reflected back to our eyes. We see black.

An orange surfboard absorbs all of the spectrum colors except orange. The orange waves are reflected back into our eyes. We see orange.

Chapter 4

Seeing Color

Humans see objects when light is reflected into our eyes.

When we look at something such as a chocolate cake, light rays bounce off the cake and enter our eyes. They pass through the cornea and into the pupil. A lens behind the pupil helps us focus on the cake. This lens also sends the light to the back wall of the eye, called the retina. The light rays form an upside-down image of the cake on the retina. The retina passes this information to the brain along the optic nerve. The brain turns the cake picture right side up, and that is the picture we see.

Colors are recognized by tiny cones and rods in the back of the eye. They send their information to the brain, too. Different cones detect different colors, while the rods pick up black and white.

The human eye

Cornea: the protective layer on the outside of the eye.

Iris: the colored ring of muscles that surround the pupil.

Retina: the back wall of the eye. The retina passes on the upside-down picture to the optic nerve.

Pupil: the opening in the eye that lets light in. The pupil becomes larger or smaller, depending on how much light it is exposed to.

Lens: the lens bends the light rays so that they form a focused picture on the retina.

Optic nerve: the nerve that transmits the information from the retina to the brain.

Did You Know?

The **cones** and **rods** that detect color are found in the retina.

Chapter 5

So You Want Pink Hair?

These days, you can dye your hair pink, green, purple, or orange, but you'll never make it grow those colors. You might wear blue contact lenses to make your eyes look bluer, but you can't make them change color permanently. That's because the natural color of our hair, eyes, and skin is determined by a chemical inside our bodies.

Contact lenses not only come in different colors, but also in different designs.

Melanin is the chemical that determines the color of our skin, hair, and eyes. When people from all around the world stand together, their coloring looks quite different. This is because their bodies produce different amounts of melanin.

Melanin is found deep in the layers of everyone's skin. As it rises toward the surface of the skin, it reacts with other chemicals. When it reaches the top layers of skin, it either gets saved by the skin **cells** or is broken down by them. People with darker skin tones have skin cells that save the melanin, while people with paler skin have cells that break it down.

Exposure to sunlight makes your skin produce extra melanin to protect itself. This is what makes pale-skinned people look tanned.

Did You Know?

Spending too much time in the sun can be harmful to your skin, as it can burn and become red and painful. Sunburn can damage skin and may lead to skin cancers. That's why it's important to apply sunscreen and wear a hat when going out in the sun.

People with brown eyes have a lot of melanin in their eyes. Brown-eyed people also tend to have more melanin in their hair, which makes it dark.

Blue-eyed people have much less melanin in their eyes. These people also tend to have less melanin in their hair and therefore often have red or blonde hair.

People with hazel eyes have a **variable** amount of melanin in their eyes. The result is a greenish eye-color. Their hair color can range from light to dark.

Chapter 6
Foods, Moods, and Marketing

Color can affect the way we feel and the choices we make. Food companies know that, so they use colors to attract us to their products.

Makers of candy and snack foods wrap their products in bright colors to make them appealing to children. Sometimes the products themselves are brightly colored.

Some food companies use natural colors in their packaging to attract people interested in buying natural, healthy foods.

Which foods would you like to eat?

Other businesses know that colors affect us, too.

Many restaurants use red to decorate their eating areas because red is said to make you feel hungry.

Yellowish-green is never used on the inside of planes because it tends to make people feel sick!

Yellow is the first color that the brain notices, so "sale" tags are often colored bright yellow. Yellow is also used for warning, such as on road signs. Today, many fire engines are painted yellow instead of red because people will see them more quickly.

Toy manufacturers know that pink is usually associated with girls. Many of their toys for girls are colored pink, while boys' toys are often shades of blue.

Hospitals use colors, too. Research studies show that patients need less medication and recover more quickly from surgery if they can see green views from their windows.

Chapter 7

The Color of the Weather Report

"Good evening viewers! Welcome to the weather report. Didn't we have some colorful weather today! To begin, did you notice the sunrise early this morning? When the sun gets close to the **horizon**, it has a much thicker layer of atmosphere to shine through than it does at lunchtime. You'll notice the yellow light waves get blocked easily by that extra bit of atmosphere. Luckily those glorious red and orange waves got through just fine and painted the sky for us. Perfect conditions for these early morning balloon enthusiasts."

Weatherman: Hugh Palette

"At noon we were lucky enough to spot a rainbow. The rain was just finishing and those sunrays were at work again. There were still many tiny water droplets in the air as the sun came out. Those droplets acted like small prisms in the air. As you know, light that passes through a prism is splintered into a spectrum. Well, that's just what happened up there, only this spectrum was so big we can call it a rainbow! What a sight!

"After the rain cleared we had a fine afternoon. All of those dust particles and water droplets in the atmosphere did a good job of splitting and scattering the spectrum colors. As usual, blue light waves were being scattered the most, so we had the pleasure of viewing blue skies for the remainder of the day.

"Tomorrow we can expect big gray rain clouds to develop after lunch. The large number of water droplets held up in those clouds will be absorbing more light than they reflect, so it will be gray skies indeed. And remember your umbrella, because those clouds are going to let loose at some point!

"Well, there you have it, the color of the weather report for today. Look outside right now and enjoy the beautiful sunset! I'll see you tomorrow for some more colorful weather."

Chapter 8

Sarah Snap's Field Notes

Field Notes for Camouflage Pics

Biologist and wildlife photographer: *Sarah Snap*

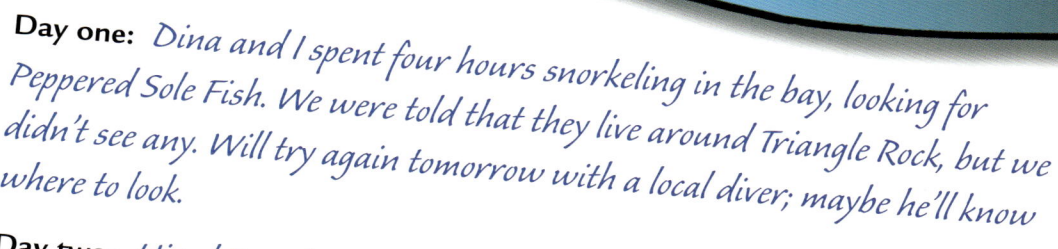

Location:

Nelson Bay

Day one: Dina and I spent four hours snorkeling in the bay, looking for Peppered Sole Fish. We were told that they live around Triangle Rock, but we didn't see any. Will try again tomorrow with a local diver; maybe he'll know where to look.

Day two: Hired Ben the Diver to show us the sole fish. Ben has been snorkeling here for 15 years and sees them often. Couldn't believe it when he took us to the exact spot we had been yesterday! When Ben pointed at the sandy bottom, I couldn't see anything. Then, something started to move and I realized it was a fish! What great camouflage: the sole was dotted with dark brown and black speckles, just like the sand. Peppered Sole is a good name for it! When it stopped moving, I had to watch carefully as it settled back into the sand. Suddenly, I noticed four more in the sand nearby. We must have swum over plenty of them yesterday, and never noticed! Got good shots for book. Hurray, this assignment is finished!

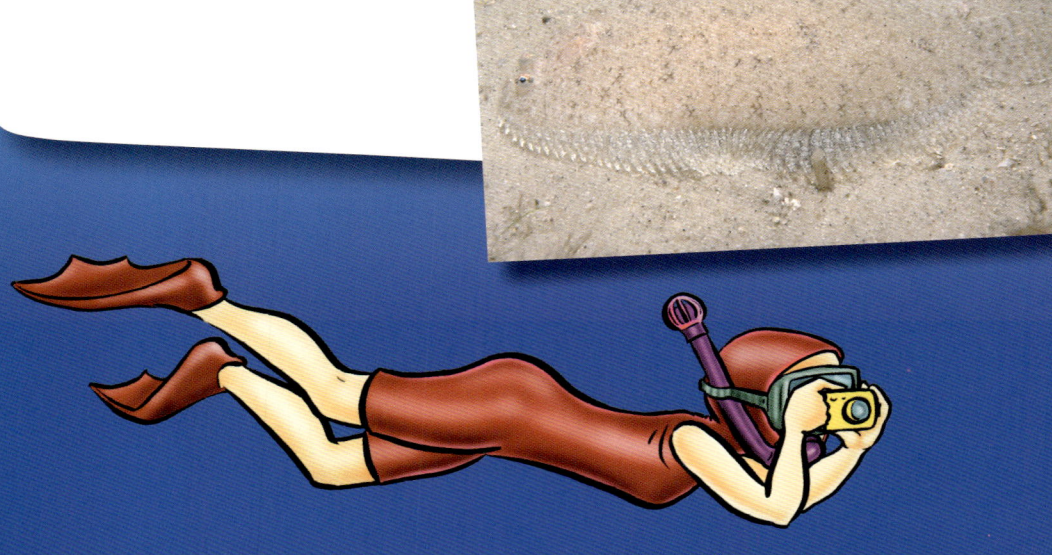

Chapter 9

At the Printer

The world may be made up of many, many different colors, but a color printer only uses four. Books, magazines, newspapers, and computer printers use just four colors to trick our eyes into seeing colors that aren't really there.

Most printers use the colors **cyan**, **magenta**, yellow, and black. These colors are printed as tiny dots on the page. The dots are arranged in a special grid pattern. None of the dots touch, but our eyes and brain blend them together so that we "see" a whole range of colors.

Glossary

absorb	to take in
cells	tiny parts of living matter
cyan	a name for a vivid color blue, used in printing
horizon	where the sky seems to meet the earth in the distance
magenta	a name for a bold pink color, used in printing
melanin	the chemical that controls the darkness of a person's skin, hair, and eyes
prism	a clear block, usually made of glass, that breaks up white light into the colors of the spectrum
reflect	to throw back light, such as a mirror does
splintered	broken apart
transmit	to send or carry one thing to another
variable	a differing amount, hard to determine